M000309920

THIS JOURNAL BELONGS TO:

_____

This journal features quotes from
the following classic novels by Jane Austen:

PRIDE AND PREJUDICE

SENSE AND SENSIBILITY

EMMA

MANSFIELD PARK

PERSUASION

NORTHANGER ABBEY

POUR YOUR HEART OUT

A JOURNAL OF WIT, WISDOM, AND A TOUCH OF CHARM

quotes by
JANE AUSTEN

illustrations by
CLARE OWEN

POUR YOUR HEART OUT

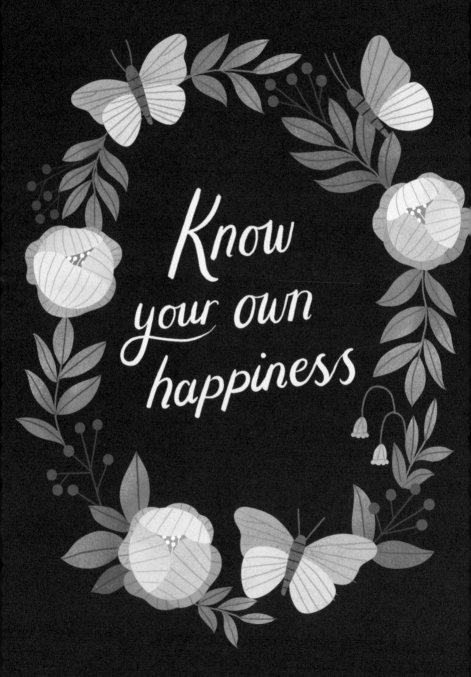

Know your own happiness

FAVORITE SNACK FOOD:

_____

FAVORITE SEASON:

_____

FAVORITE COLOR:

_____

FAVORITE BOOK:

_____

FAVORITE MOVIE:

_____

FAVORITE TV SHOW:

_____

FAVORITE KEEPSAKE:

_____

FAVORITE PLACE:

_____

FAVORITE PERSON:

_____

Let's have no
SECRETS AMONG FRIENDS.

What would your friends be surprised to find out about you?

A FONDNESS FOR READING,

WHICH, PROPERLY DIRECTED, MUST BE AN EDUCATION IN ITSELF.

Check off the books you've read. Star the ones you want to
read next. If your favorites are missing, add them here!

Let's start with the obvious:

☐ *Pride and Prejudice* (Jane Austen)
☐ *Sense and Sensibility* (Jane Austen)
☐ *Emma* (Jane Austen)
☐ *Mansfield Park* (Jane Austen)
☐ *Persuasion* (Jane Austen)
☐ *Northanger Abbey* (Jane Austen)

☐ *Little Women* (Louisa May Alcott)
☐ *Wuthering Heights* (Emily Brontë)
☐ *Jane Eyre* (Charlotte Brontë)
☐ *The Adventures of Huckleberry Finn* (Mark Twain)
☐ *Middlemarch* (George Eliot)
☐ *Robinson Crusoe* (Daniel Defoe)
☐ *The Swiss Family Robinson* (Johann David Wyss)
☐ *The Scarlet Letter* (Nathaniel Hawthorne)
☐ *Alice's Adventures in Wonderland* (Lewis Carroll)
☐ *Treasure Island* (Robert Louis Stevenson)
☐ *Romeo and Juliet* (William Shakespeare)
☐ *To Kill a Mockingbird* (Harper Lee)
☐ *Anne of Green Gables* (L. M. Montgomery)
☐ *The Call of the Wild* (Jack London)

_____

_____

_____

_____

_____

_____

_____

_____

_____

It is very often

nothing but our

own vanity that

deceives us.

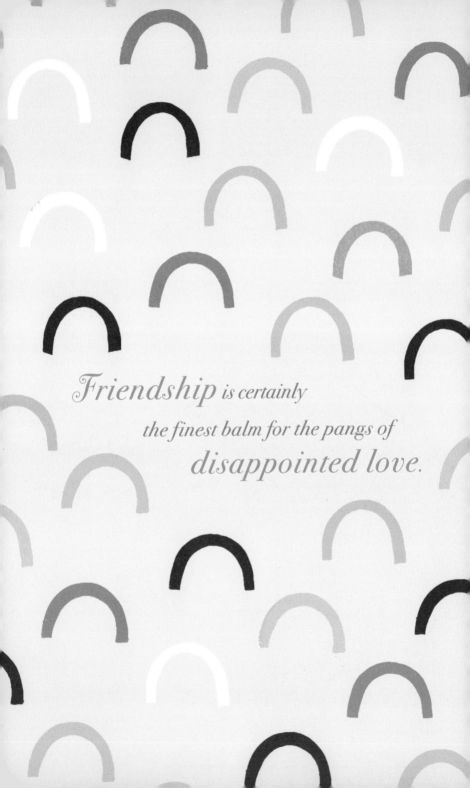

Friendship is certainly the finest balm for the pangs of disappointed love.

What else is in your "feel better" kit?

HIS HORROR

OF LATE HOURS

AND LARGE

DINNER-PARTIES

MADE HIM

UNFIT FOR ANY

ACQUAINTANCE.

Are you an early bird or a night owl?

Try being the opposite for one day and write down what you did!

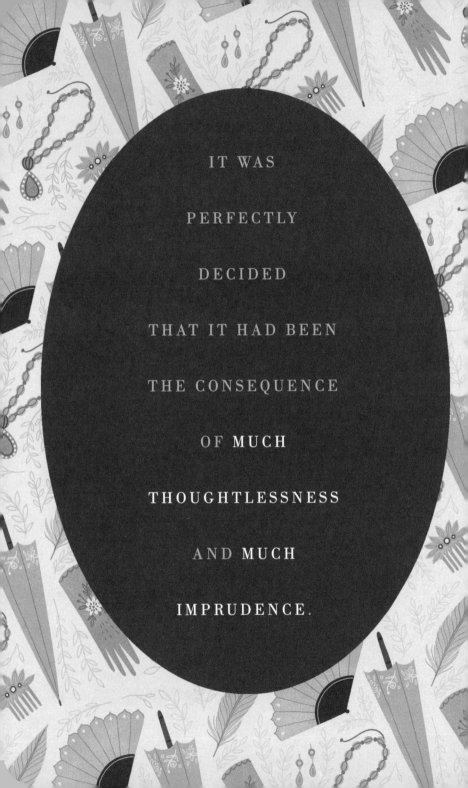

IT WAS

PERFECTLY

DECIDED

THAT IT HAD BEEN

THE CONSEQUENCE

OF MUCH

THOUGHTLESSNESS

AND MUCH

IMPRUDENCE.

What was your latest impulse buy?

Was it worth it? Why or why not?

Nothing could now be clearer than the absurdity of her recent fancies.

Receipt for guilty pleasures:

ONE WILL NEVER
TEASE THE OTHER
BEYOND WHAT
IS KNOWN TO BE
PLEASANT.

What's the one thing you can't live down?

IF YOU ARE EVER SO

FORWARD AND CLEVER

YOURSELVES, YOU SHOULD

ALWAYS BE MODEST;

FOR, MUCH AS YOU

KNOW ALREADY, THERE

IS A GREAT DEAL MORE

FOR YOU TO LEARN.

Things you know too much about:

Things you want to learn more about:

HOW
QUICK
COME THE
REASONS
FOR
APPROVING
WHAT WE
LIKE!

List your most convincing arguments for indulging.

_____

_____

_____

_____

_____

_____

_____

_____

_____

_____

_____

_____

A WATCH IS ALWAYS *too fast* OR *too slow.* I CANNOT BE DICTATED TO BY A *watch.*

Moments you wish time moved slower:

Moments you wish time moved faster:

Her feelings were very acute,
and too little understood to
be properly attended to.

Nobody meant to be unkind,
but nobody put themselves out of
their way to secure *her comfort*.

Perform one random act of kindness every day
for a week. Write them down here.

SUNDAY:

_____

MONDAY:

_____

TUESDAY:

_____

WEDNESDAY:

_____

THURSDAY:

_____

FRIDAY:

_____

SATURDAY:

_____

IT WAS MUCH
EASIER TO CHAT
THAN TO STUDY.

What are the worst distractions when you're trying to concentrate?

How do you tune them out?

There is
nothing so bad as
parting
with one's
friends.

Who is the one person you'd miss the most?

List the five things you'd miss about them.

1. _____

_____

2. _____

_____

3. _____

_____

4. _____

_____

5. _____

_____

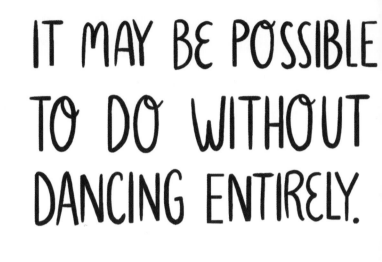

IT MAY BE POSSIBLE
TO DO WITHOUT
DANCING ENTIRELY.

What other "fun things" can you live without?

I AM NOT TO BE
INTIMIDATED
INTO ANYTHING
SO WHOLLY
UNREASONABLE.

Describe a time when you were peer pressured.

FOR A FEW
MOMENTS HER
imagination

AND
HER
heart

No.9

WERE
bewitched.

My ideas flow so rapidly that I have not time to express them.

Without lifting your pen from the paper, fill the page with anything and everything that comes to mind.

WE SEEM SO

BESET WITH DIFFICULTIES

ON EVERY SIDE,

THAT THOUGH IT WOULD

MAKE US MISERABLE

FOR A TIME,

WE SHOULD BE HAPPIER

PERHAPS IN THE END.

List three difficulties you're facing right now.

1. _____

2. _____

3. _____

What do you hope is the light at the end of the tunnel?

Every profession is necessary and honourable in its turn.

What were your three easiest jobs?

1. _____

2. _____

3. _____

What were your three most difficult jobs?

1. _____

2. _____

3. _____

Which of your jobs did you learn the most from?

Songs
and proverbs,
all talk of ,
women's
fickleness.

But perhaps
you will say,
these were all
written by
men.

What do you wish you understood about the opposite sex?

What do you wish they knew about you?

ALL MANNER OF SOLEMN NONSENSE WAS TALKED ON THE SUBJECT, BUT I BELIEVED NONE OF IT.

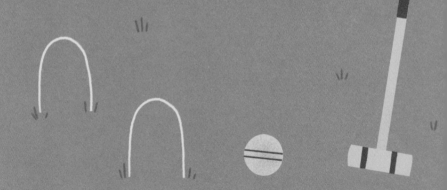

Pick a topic, any topic, and argue against your own opinion.

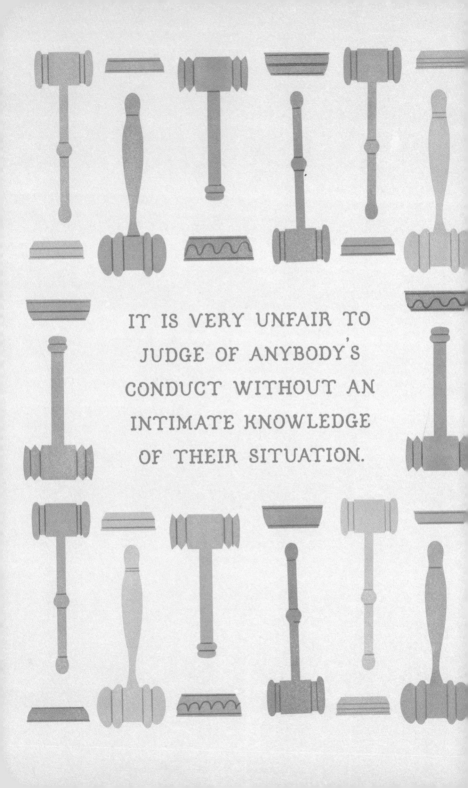

IT IS VERY UNFAIR TO
JUDGE OF ANYBODY'S
CONDUCT WITHOUT AN
INTIMATE KNOWLEDGE
OF THEIR SITUATION.

Has someone ever made an unfair assumption about you?

What do you wish you could tell them?

I HAVE
BEEN USED TO
CONSIDER
POETRY
AS THE *FOOD*
OF LOVE.

Plan a romantic four-course meal. What's on the menu?

APPETIZER:

SALAD:

MAIN COURSE:

DRINK:

DESSERT:

SURPRISES ARE FOOLISH THINGS.
THE PLEASURE IS NOT ENHANCED,
AND THE INCONVENIENCE IS
OFTEN CONSIDERABLE.

How do you feel about surprises? Love 'em? Hate 'em?
Do you prefer to be on the receiving end or the giving end?

List the pros and cons here.

PROS

CONS

Till this moment, I never knew myself.

What have you discovered about yourself over the past year?

SHE EXPECTED FROM
OTHER PEOPLE THE
SAME OPINIONS AND
FEELINGS AS HER OWN, AND
SHE JUDGED OF THEIR MOTIVES
BY THE IMMEDIATE EFFECT
OF THEIR ACTIONS
ON HERSELF.

Think about the last blowout fight you had—now put yourself in the other person's shoes. Has your viewpoint changed?

SHE ENDEAVOURED TO

FORGET WHAT SHE COULD

NOT OVERLOOK.

What are your relationship dealbreakers?

WHERE
THE MIND
IS PERHAPS
RATHER
UNWILLING
TO BE
CONVINCED,
IT WILL
ALWAYS FIND
SOMETHING
TO SUPPORT
ITS DOUBTS.

Something giving you doubts? List all your concerns here.

_____

_____

_____

_____

_____

_____

_____

_____

_____

_____

_____

_____

_____

If a woman

doubts as to

whether she

should accept

a man or not,

she certainly…

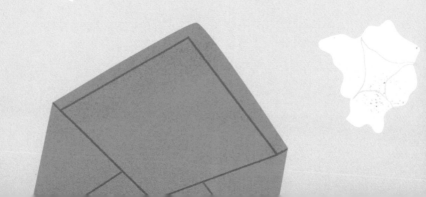

...ought to refuse him.

WEDDING-CAKE
MIGHT CERTAINLY DISAGREE
WITH MANY—PERHAPS WITH
MOST PEOPLE—UNLESS TAKEN
MODERATELY.

What's the one food you would not want to eat in moderation?

Write down the very best recipe.

*What one
means one day,
you know,
one may not mean
the next.*

*Circumstances
change,
opinions
alter.*

Write a letter to your younger self.
What advice would you give them?

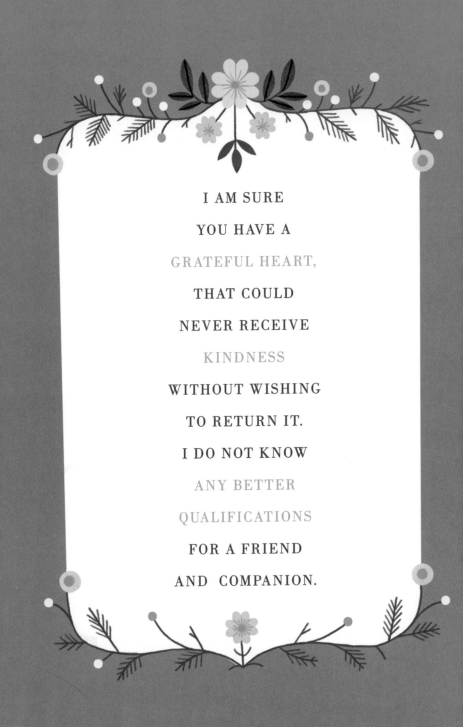

I AM SURE

YOU HAVE A

GRATEFUL HEART,

THAT COULD

NEVER RECEIVE

KINDNESS

WITHOUT WISHING

TO RETURN IT.

I DO NOT KNOW

ANY BETTER

QUALIFICATIONS

FOR A FRIEND

AND COMPANION.

Write a job description for the ideal friend.

SHE WAS STRONGER ALONE.

What do you do in your "me time"?

How do these things make you stronger?

VANITY

WORKING ON
A WEAK HEAD
PRODUCES
EVERY SORT
OF MISCHIEF.

Got big plans in your future?
Check yourself before you wreck yourself:

Is it legal?

Can you afford it?

Is it going to hurt someone physically or emotionally?

Is this really a good idea?

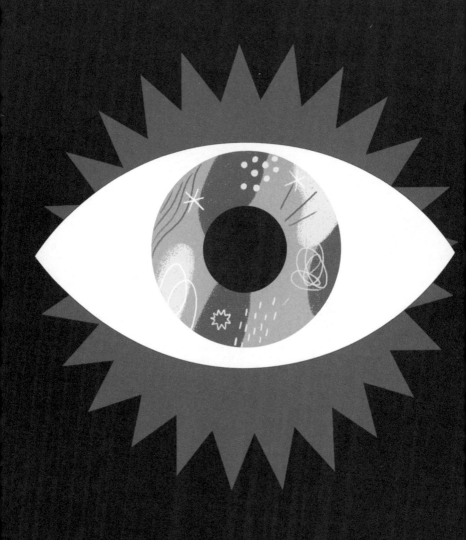

Imagination supplied

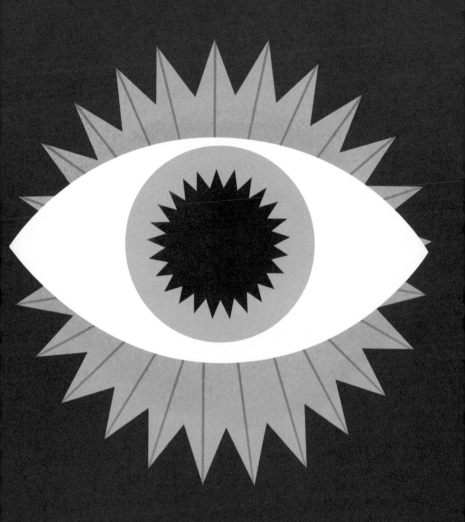

what the eye could not reach.

A GOOD MEMORY IS UNPARDONABLE.

Someday I'll look back and still be mad about:

It is such
a happiness
when good
people
get together—
and they
always do.

Who would you ship and why? (Fictional or real.)

Nobody who
has not been in
the interior of a
family can say what
the difficulties of
any individual
of that family
may be.

My crazy life:

GOOD CRAZY | BAD CRAZY

*He never wished
to attach me.
It was merely
a blind to
conceal his real
situation
with another.*

What was the last relationship (romantic or otherwise) that disappointed you? How did you handle it?

ONE

MUST NOT

EXPECT

EVERY-

THING.

Make a wish list of all the things you
want for your birthday/the holidays.

Then circle the non-negotiables.

_____

_____

_____

_____

_____

_____

_____

_____

_____

_____

_____

_____

_____

WICKEDNESS

IS ALWAYS

wickedness,

BUT FOLLY

IS NOT ALWAYS

folly.

Think about a time when a joke went too far.
What were the consequences?

Every day confirms my
belief of the inconsistency
of all human characters.

What's the most out-of-character thing you've ever done?

How did it make you feel?

ONE MAN'S WAYS

MAY BE AS GOOD

AS ANOTHER'S,

BUT WE ALL

LIKE OUR

OWN BEST.

MOST LIKELY TO _____ : ME

BEST _____ : ME

#1 _____ : ME

BIGGEST _____ : ME

MOST _____ : ME

WHAT IS PASSABLE IN YOUTH IS DETESTABLE IN LATER AGE.

What bad habits did you have that you can no longer get away with? Have you picked up any new habits?

TO WISH WAS
TO HOPE AND,
TO HOPE WAS
TO EXPECT.

Blow out the candles. What's your wish?

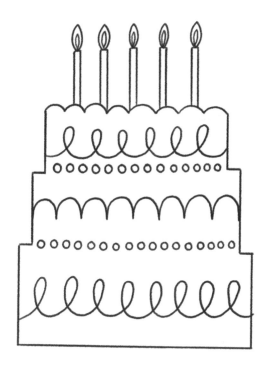

Where the heart is really attached,

I KNOW VERY WELL HOW LITTLE ONE CAN BE PLEASED WITH THE ATTENTION OF ANYONE ELSE.

What fills up your heart?

Such weather
makes every thing
and every body
disgusting.

Plan your rainy day schedule.

MORNING:

AFTERNOON:

NIGHT:

YOUNG
PEOPLE
WILL BE
YOUNG
PEOPLE,

AS YOUR GOOD MOTHER
SAYS HERSELF.

I really hate it when my mom/dad/sibling says:

How do you show someone that you care?

Now go do it!

THERE IS NOTHING I WOULD NOT

DO FOR THOSE WHO ARE REALLY

MY FRIENDS. I HAVE NO NOTION

OF LOVING PEOPLE BY HALVES;

IT IS NOT MY NATURE.

What are the craziest things you would do for a friend?

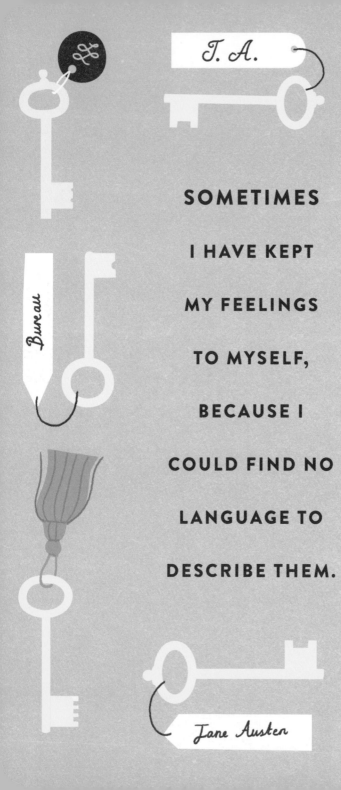

SOMETIMES
I HAVE KEPT
MY FEELINGS
TO MYSELF,
BECAUSE I
COULD FIND NO
LANGUAGE TO
DESCRIBE THEM.

Jane Austen

Draw (or paste pictures of) the objects you feel represent you metaphorically.

It was
necessary
to laugh,
when
she would
rather
have
cried.

List the things that make you laugh!
(Person, joke, movie, TV show, book, memory,
pop-culture moment, website, meme...)

Have you
never known
the pleasure
and triumph
of a lucky guess?

Make three predictions for the future.

TOMORROW:

NEXT MONTH:

NEXT YEAR:

FACTS *or* OPINIONS

which are to pass through the hands of so many...

CAN HARDLY HAVE MUCH TRUTH LEFT.

What was the most outrageous rumor you've heard lately?

Their straightforward emotions

left no room for

the little zigzags

of embarrassment.

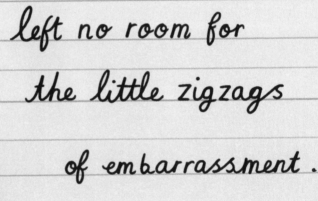

If you could tell your crush outright how you feel, what would you say? Write out the dialogue here.

YOU:

_____

_____

_____

THEM:

_____

_____

_____

YOU:

_____

_____

_____

THEM:

_____

_____

_____

ANGRY PEOPLE ARE NOT ALWAYS WISE

What's a decision you've made in anger that you now regret?

She CANNOT EXPECT

to excel, if she does not

PRACTISE A GREAT DEAL.

What about yourself can you improve on?

Create a five-step program for how to do it.

1. _____

   _____

2. _____

   _____

3. _____

   _____

4. _____

   _____

5. _____

   _____

SHE HAD DONE NOTHING
WHICH WOMAN'S FRIENDSHIP
AND WOMAN'S FEELINGS
WOULD NOT JUSTIFY.

Who would you want on your squad? (Real, fictional, celebrity.)

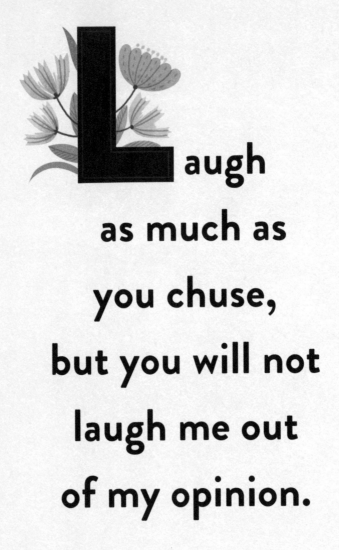

Laugh
as much as
you chuse,
but you will not
laugh me out
of my opinion.

Describe a time when you had the unpopular opinion.
Did you stay quiet or make your feelings heard?

It was
impossible
for her
to say
what she
did not
feel.

If you don't have anything nice to say . . . say it here!

A lady's imagination

is very rapid; it jumps from
admiration to love,
from love to matrimony,
in a moment.

If you could plan your future, what would it include?
(In the next day, week, month, year?)

My spirits might often lead me wrong

Describe a time when doing the right thing
ended up being the wrong thing.

My vanity

was flattered,

and I allowed

his attentions.

Write down everything you never tire hearing about yourself.

These were
charming feelings,
but not lasting.

Write about a relationship that didn't pan out.

As soon as I saw you,
I felt almost as if
you was an old
acquaintance.

Who is your celebrity kindred spirit?

What do you have in common?

MY COURAGE ALWAYS
RISES WITH EVERY ATTEMPT
TO INTIMIDATE ME.

What are your techniques for overcoming intimidation?
Give yourself a pep talk!

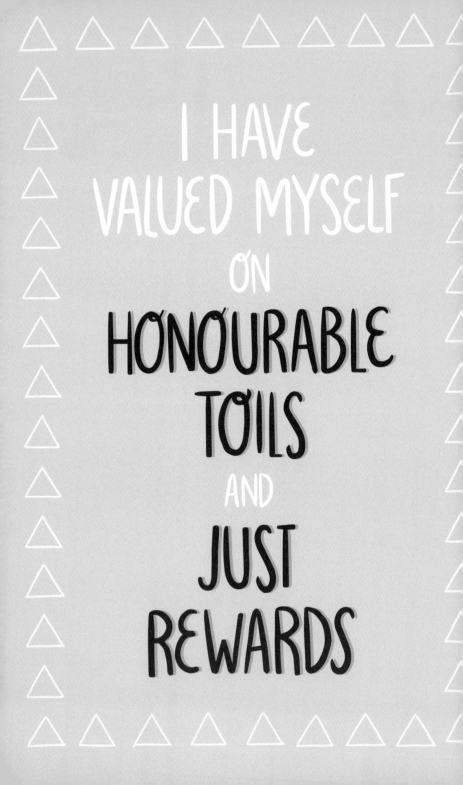

What are your just rewards?

How did you earn them?

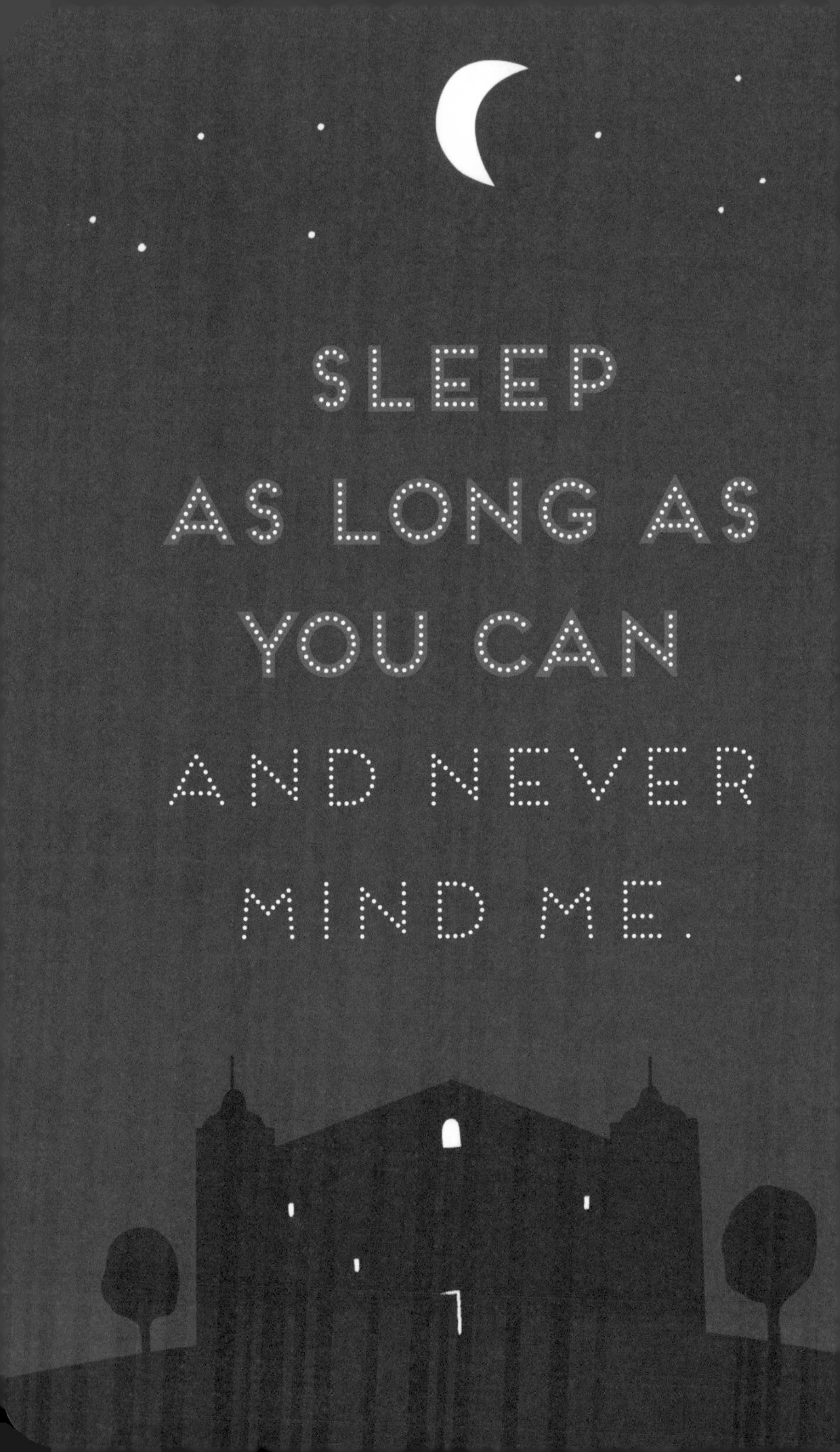
SLEEP
AS LONG AS
YOU CAN
AND NEVER
MIND ME.

Rank these in order of importance in your life:

_____ FOOD

_____ LOVE

_____ SLEEP

_____ FRIENDS

_____ FAMILY

_____ KNOWLEDGE

_____ MONEY

_____ ME-TIME

_____ SOCIAL LIFE

_____ HOBBIES

My feelings

are not often **shared,** not often **understood.**

But *sometimes* they are.

What do you think people misunderstand the most about you?

THOSE WHO
DO NOT
COMPLAIN
ARE NEVER
PITIED.

Celebrate your pity party! List all your current complaints.

_____

_____

_____

_____

_____

_____

_____

_____

_____

_____

_____

_____

_____

ONE-HALF

OF THE

WORLD

CANNOT

UNDERSTAND

THE

PLEASURES

OF THE

OTHER.

Things you like:

Things you both like:

Things your friend likes:

Her heart

was so

heavy

that no farther

sadness

could be gained.

Pour your heart out with the things that are weighing you down.

Emma watched

her through the

fluctuations of

this speech and

saw no alarming

symptoms of love.

Swoon checklist—circle all that apply:

CLAMMY HANDS

POUNDING HEART

INCESSANT GIGGLES

OBSESSIVE INTERNET STALKING

OVERACTIVE EMOTIONS

EUPHORIA

UNINTELLIGIBLE SPEECH

INSOMNIA

Time will explain

Things you didn't understand as a kid:

Things you still don't get now:

YOU ARE
DETERMINED,
I SEE, TO
HAVE NO
CURIOSITY.

Would you rather have someone know nothing
about you or everything about you?

Describe the pros and cons of each situation.

PROS | CONS

I do not
pretend to
set people
right,

but I do
see that they
are often
wrong.

THE FOLLY
OF PEOPLE'S
NOT STAYING
COMFORTABLY
AT HOME WHEN
THEY CAN!

Describe your perfect night in.

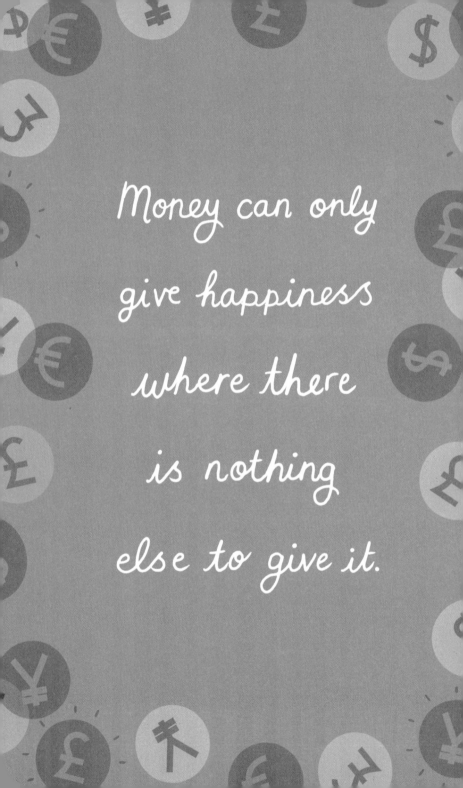

Money can only give happiness where there is nothing else to give it.

Try to go an afternoon without spending money. What did you do?

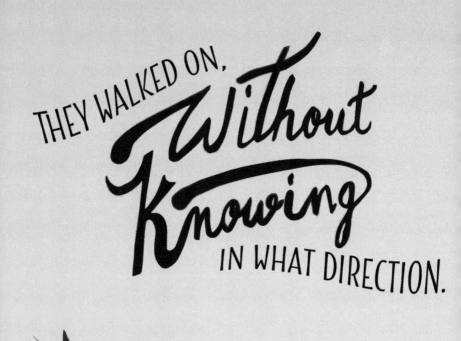

THEY WALKED ON, *Without Knowing* IN WHAT DIRECTION.

If you could find out what your future looks
like, would you want to know?

Why or why not?

You must be
the best judge
of your own
happiness.

What do people suggest you do to be happy?

Do those things actually make you happy?

Nothing ever
fatigues me,
but doing what
I do not like.

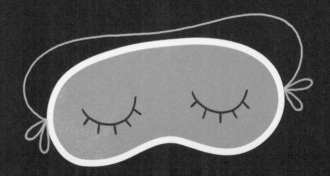

Write a list of things you've done that you
never want to experience again.

_____

_____

_____

_____

_____

_____

_____

_____

_____

_____

_____

_____

Now, how were his sentiments to be read?

Think of a time when someone sent you some confusing signals. What do you think they meant?

What did they actually mean?

With
a book
he was
regardless
of time.

What's on your reading list?

_____

_____

_____

_____

_____

_____

_____

_____

_____

_____

_____

_____

_____

_____

Think
only of
the past
as its
remembrance
gives you
pleasure.

What's your happiest memory to date?

171

WHERE
THE WOUND
HAD BEEN
GIVEN,
THERE MUST
THE CURE
BE FOUND.

What's the worst thing you've done to someone recently?

How would you make it better?

Do you know why you did it?

Selfishness

must always be forgiven you know, because there is no hope

of a cure.

What are your guidelines for forgiveness?

How long do you hold a grudge?

What's the longest you've gone without forgiving?

THE

COMFORT

AND EASE OF

FAMILIARITY

WOULD COME

IN TIME.

What does it take for you to feel comfortable
with someone or something?

She could not
endure that such
a friendship
as theirs should be
severed unfairly.

Is there a friend you don't talk to anymore?

What was the reason for the "breakup"?

WOMAN

IS FINE FOR HER OWN

SATISFACTION ALONE.

NO MAN

WILL ADMIRE HER THE MORE,

NO WOMAN WILL LIKE HER

THE BETTER FOR IT.

Draw one item from your wardrobe that makes you feel like a total badass, or paste a picture of you wearing it here!

She was tired of
being continually
pressed against
by people, the
generality of whose
faces possessed
nothing to interest,
and with all of whom
she was so wholly
unacquainted.

When was the last time you found yourself in a
crowded space (party, concert, etc.)?

Would you consider it a positive or negative experience?

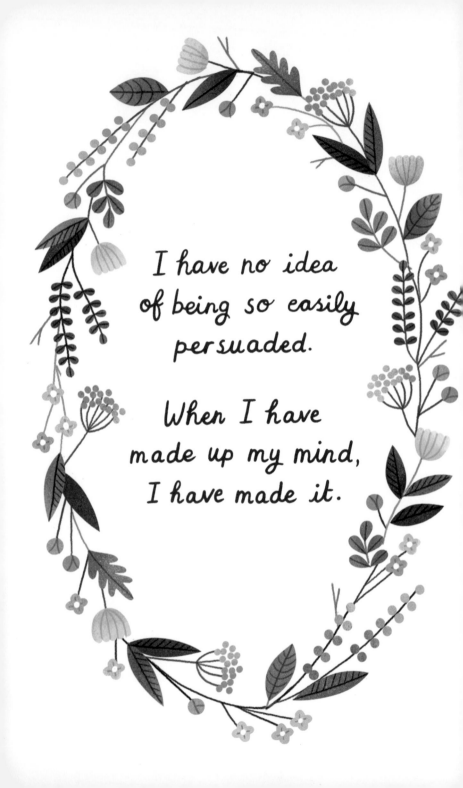

I have no idea
of being so easily
persuaded.

When I have
made up my mind,
I have made it.

Having trouble making an important decision?

List the pros and cons.

PROS | CONS

Better be without sense than misapply it as you do.

List your silliest mistakes.

_____

_____

_____

_____

_____

_____

_____

_____

_____

_____

_____

_____

_____

YOUR OWN JUDGMENT MUST DIRECT YOU.

If you were emperor of the world, what
would you outlaw for all time?

What new laws would you create?

*She had talked
her into love;
but alas!*

*she was not
so easily to be
talked out of it.*

Do you find it easier to fall in or out of love? Why?

When a young lady is
to be *a heroine*

. . . something must
and will happen to
throw *a hero* in her way.

List three small acts of heroism you've done over the last year.

1. _____

_____

_____

_____

2. _____

_____

_____

_____

3. _____

_____

_____

_____

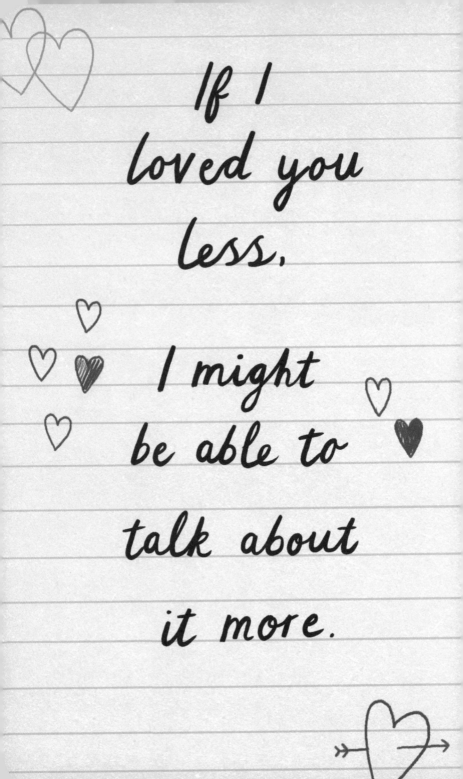

Talk about it all you want here!

NONE
OF US
EXPECT
TO BE IN
SMOOTH
WATER
ALL OUR
DAYS.

What challenges have you overcome in the past
that will help you face future challenges?

My idea of
good company ...
is the company of
clever, well-informed
people, who have
a great deal
of conversation;

that is what i call
good company.

If you were a talk show host, who would you invite as guests on your show?

Her mind received knowledge which had never before fallen in her way

You learn something new every day!

SUNDAY:

_____

MONDAY:

_____

TUESDAY:

_____

WEDNESDAY:

_____

THURSDAY:

_____

FRIDAY:

_____

SATURDAY:

_____

*Her heart was sore and angry,
and she was capable only
of angry consolations.*

Color your heart out.

PENGUIN BOOKS
An imprint of Penguin Random House LLC
375 Hudson Street
New York, New York 10014

First published in the United States of America by Penguin Books,
an imprint of Penguin Random House LLC, 2018

Cover and interior art copyright © 2018 by Clare Owen
Interior design by Samira Iravani and Jessica Jenkins

Penguin Books ISBN 9780425290583

Printed in China

1 3 5 7 9 10 8 6 4 2

JANE AUSTEN (December 1775–July 1817) was an English novelist whose works of romantic fiction have earned her a place as one of the most widely read and most beloved writers in English literature. She started writing *Pride and Prejudice* when she was only twenty-two years old, and though it was initially rejected by the publisher she submitted it to, it eventually published in 1813 after much revision. In addition to *Pride and Prejudice*, she is also the author of *Sense and Sensibility*, *Mansfield Park*, *Emma*, *Northanger Abbey*, and *Persuasion*.

CLARE OWEN is a British illustrator from the Southwest of England. When not illustrating, Clare can be found cycling, reading, and cooing at cute dogs.

clareowen.com
@clarelpowen